LET'S EXPLORE NORTH AMERICA

(MOST FAMOUS ATTRACTIONS IN NORTH AMERICA)

Speedy Publishing LLC
40 E. Main St. #1156
Newark, DE 19711
www.speedypublishing.com

North America is the third largest continent by area. North America has many exciting destinations to visit.

Banff National Park is located in the south western corner of the province of Alberta in Canada's Rocky Mountains. Banff National Park is Canada's oldest national park. Banff National Park is one of the most visited national parks in North America.

The Niagara Falls are made up of 3 waterfalls, the American Falls, the Bridal Veil Falls and the Horseshoe Falls. The Horseshoe Falls are the largest and the Bridal Veil Falls the smallest.

Big Sur is located along Scenic Highway One approximately 150 miles south of San Francisco and 300 miles north of Los Angeles. Besides sightseeing from the highway, Big Sur offers hiking, mountain climbing, and other outdoor activities.

Yellowstone National Park is a national park located primarily in the U.S. state of Wyoming. Yellowstone is the world's first National Park.

JULY
IV

The Statue of Liberty is a colossal neoclassical sculpture on Liberty Island in New York Harbor in New York City. The female form represented by the sculpture is based on Libertas, the Roman goddess of liberty.

The Golden Gate Bridge links the northern tip of the San Francisco Peninsula to Marin County. The bridge is one of the most internationally recognized symbols of San Francisco.

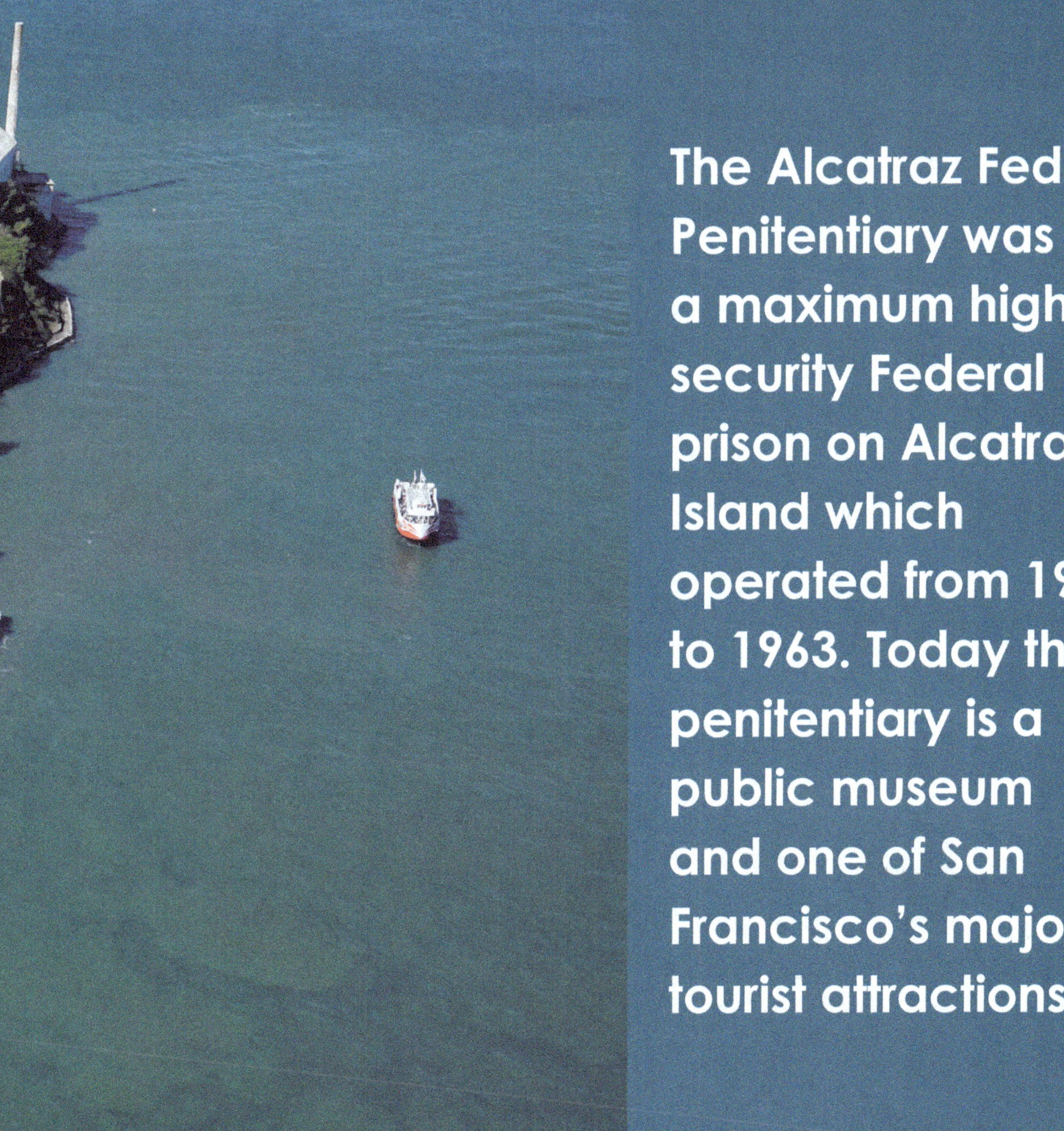

The Alcatraz Federal Penitentiary was a maximum high-security Federal prison on Alcatraz Island which operated from 1934 to 1963. Today the penitentiary is a public museum and one of San Francisco's major tourist attractions.

www.ingramcontent.com/pod-product-compliance
Lightning Source LLC
LaVergne TN
LVHW060515170826
845677LV00026B/1764

* 9 7 9 8 8 6 9 4 5 1 9 4 1 *